W.I.N.N.

Against

Suicide

by

Robert E. Nelson Jr., Ph.D.

R&E Publishers
Saratoga, California

R & E Publishers
P.O. Box 2008, Saratoga, CA 95070
Tel: (408) 866-6303   Fax: (408) 866-0825

Book design by Diane Parker

Cover by Kaye Quinn

Library of Congress Card Cataloging-in-Publication Data

ISBN 1-56875-049-8

1. Suicide—Prevention 2. Suicide—Psychological aspects. 3. Suicide. 4. Counseling. I. Title. II. Title: WINN against suicide.

HV6545.N45 1993   93-27963
362.2'87--dc20   CIP

Contents

Introduction

Most of us have heard the theme song from the television program and movie, *M.A.S.H.,* that includes the words "suicide is painless". Perhaps nothing could be more untrue.

I have been a high school counselor, mental health counselor, military chaplain, and private practitioner. Over the years, I have counseled the suicidal, buried the suicides, and comforted their loved ones. One thing I have learned for sure: suicide is not painless. It is painful at every stage. It is born of pain and fulfilled in pain. It creates pain in the lives of those it touches.

Over the past few years, I have taught suicide prevention classes to thousands of people. These classes have saved lives. Some of these lives I know for sure. I am sure there are others as well that have been saved and will be saved because of the tools learned and the awareness gained.

To help increase awareness of the basics of suicide prevention I developed the acronym **W.I.N.N.** for *Watch, Integrate, and Never.* To *watch* is to be aware of those around us. It is to become more sensitive to their feelings and their actions. To *integrate* is to make people feel that they belong. It is to be friendly, caring and loving. And, we must *never* ignore threats of suicide. *Never* take it lightly. *Never* leave the potential suicide alone. *Never* give them access to the means of suicide. And *never* keep a deadly secret.

These few basics can save lives.

Suicide is tragic. It is a waste of life. It is the opposite of hope. It is despair and loneliness and guilt. It is final and total. It is destruction. It is a great, dark evil but it is not inevitable or invincible.

We can defeat it. We can begin by decreasing its opportunities. We can increase our understanding of what it is. We can give hope. We can draw together. We can build trust, togetherness, and self-esteem. We can win against suicide. And that is the message of this book.

Robert E. Nelson Jr.
1993

1 The Problem

I took a suicide call late one night while working at a crisis center in California. Rhonda (not her real name) was crying and upset and said she just wanted to talk. Then she told me that she had just taken a whole bottle of Valium and she was also threatening to cut her wrists. I kept her on the phone while my co-workers attempted to trace the call. Her speech was becoming slurred as the Valium took effect.

At one point I managed to get an address from her but she remained despondent.

"Nobody cares," she said.

"I care, Rhonda."

She was tearful. The conversation repeated as I tried to keep her talking. She became increasingly incoherent. Her speech became softer and more slurred and confused. Then she was silent.

I could hear her moving—not in an organized manner but in a random, confused fashion like someone fitfully sleeping on the floor. She bumped the phone. Then even the movement stopped.

I stayed on the line hoping that I might hear the police arrive. My co-workers continued the phone trace in case she had lied about the address. As I waited I could hear the television in the background where her boyfriend sat in another room ignorant of what was happening. There was the sound of a baby crying. Once again I heard a sound as though someone had jerked or rolled and hit the phone.

Then I heard a tragic, ironic monologue. It was the voice of a man—probably the boy friend:

"Rhonda, did you call a ****ing ambulance?"

Then louder, angrily: "What the **** is going on here?"

Then there was the sound of the telephone receiver being returned to its cradle.

Later the sheriff's department called to let me know that Rhonda had been taken to a hospital. She was alive.

How would you be feeling right now if this story was about your daughter, your wife, or a friend? I have had the opportunity of teaching suicide prevention classes to thousands of people. At the beginning of the class I usually ask for a show of hands of all those who have had a member of their family, a friend, or a close acquaintance like a co-worker or fellow student attempt or "succeed" at suicide. Usually anywhere from one-third to a half of the class will raise their hands. Then I explain that for those who didn't raise their hands they would most likely be able to if we were to come back in ten years and ask the question again.

Suicide is common. It touches our lives. It is in the top five to ten causes of death in most European countries and in North America. More than half a million Americans between fifteen and twenty-four attempt suicide every year.

You already know a lot about suicide. Perhaps you can raise your hand as one whose life has been touched by this tragedy. Maybe you have thought about it or even attempted it yourself. At the very least you know about it because it is in the newspaper, on television, in the movies, in life.

Suicide is a problem. It is the loss of life. It is the killing of the future and hope. Suicide is the act of one person that stabs at the heart of us all.

In the next few chapters we'll take a closer look at suicide and we'll learn a few tools to help us defend ourselves and our loved ones.

2 The Myth

Suicide is so common that we all know a lot about it. The problem is that when we know a lot about something a certain amount of what we know isn't true. For example, we all know that Columbus was the first to figure out that the world was round instead of flat only it's not true. We all know that the birds fly south for the winter only it's not true (if you think it is then take a look around and see how many birds you can see this winter). Let's look at a few of the things we "know" about suicide.

You'd have to be crazy to kill yourself.

Not really. Although some people who commit suicide are psychotic, the vast majority are not what most of us would consider "crazy". They don't do bizarre things, hear voices, or see things. They don't think they are Napoleon or that aliens are spying on them. They are people like you and me who are, for whatever reasons, having thoughts and impulses concerning the taking of their own lives.

Someone might say that anyone who wants to take his or her own life is "crazy". If you want to define it that way then you're right. But if you mean that that person is the victim of some kind of mental or emotional "illness" then the term doesn't apply. Although many suicidal people may also suffer from clinical depression they don't necessarily meet the criteria that is used to diagnose a person as psychotic. Depressed is not the same thing as crazy. Abraham Lincoln for example, suffered a major depressive episode and was prone to extreme depression even while president, but was he crazy? Probably no one but the most ardent Jeff Davis supporter would think so. Compulsive thoughts about suicide may in fact be quite normal given the right circumstances. Such thoughts are more indicative of a person who is trapped and sees no way out of a hopeless situation than they are of someone who is simply not in touch with reality.

In fact, virtually all of us at some time or other will think of suicide. Everyone who becomes depressed will think about it. And everyone is going to be depressed at some time. We probably won't say anything about it to anyone because we will feel guilty or embarrassed. Suicide is almost a bad word. It's just not the kind of thing we can easily talk about. But how many times have you or someone you know said, "I might as well kill myself." These words or words like them even when not said with lethal intent are evidence that we normal people (whatever that means) do think of suicide. Fortunately, most of the time it goes no further than that. The thoughts are not compulsive and continuous. But given the wrong kind of situation for the right amount of time even you and I could be at risk.

Suicide is hereditary.

While it's true that there are some examples of generations of suicides (for example, Ernest Hemingway, his father and son) suicide can and does strike in families that haven't had a suicide in generations. This myth comes from drawing conclusions from too little data. The statistics just don't bear it out. It just isn't so. Suicide is not a biological thing that can be inherited.

Someone who is reading this book may disagree. You may know of a family that has many suicides: father, son, grandson. From this you might conclude that suicide is inherited. But you may also have had bad luck once after a black cat crossed your path. Do you believe that black cats are unlucky? Some people do and no matter what I say they will not be dissuaded.

A similar phenomenon is the "full moon" syndrome. Ask any emergency room worker or obstetrics nurse and they will tell you that there are more emergencies and more childbirths on a night with a full moon than on other nights. It's one of those things that everybody knows. If you go over the records you'll find it is just not true but still everybody knows it. It's a case of only noticing the evidence that backs up what you already believe.

In some cases it may be a self-fulfilling prophecy. I once worked with a woman who believed strongly in astrology. She would particularly note the days when Mercury was in retrograde. On those days she expected things to go wrong and she could not rest until they did. No matter how minor the problem—a misspelled word, a spilled cup of coffee, or even a slip of the tongue—she would point out that it was because Mercury was in retrograde. She would often be the cause of the mistake but Mercury got the blame. We are all that way to some extent. If we believe something has to be we'll even work to make it so. Mark Twain entered the world with Halley's comet and believed he would exit when the comet came again. He did. Yes, even death can be a self-fulfilling prophecy.

But in general we do not find evidence of suicide running in families. It happens once in a while but the facts don't bear it out as a general rule.

Only certain types of people are the suicidal type.

There is no "suicide type". It could be a quiet scholar or a slap-on-the-back jock. It can happen to rich or poor, male or female, young or old. It includes all occupations and all religions. Suicides have included outgoing macho men like Ernest Hemingway and professional academics like Bruno Bettelheim. While it is true that there are people who are at greater risk, the risk factors are more a matter of situation than of type. For example, few would consider a powerful, successful attorney to be a likely candidate for suicide. But what if that same attorney were found to be guilty of a serious crime and were about to lose his family, his career, his reputation, and his freedom? By the same token the poor farmer who barely scratches a living from the dirt might be considered by some to be a more likely candidate for suicide. Yet he might live a long life undisturbed by any thought of suicide surrounded by family and friends who fret the weather and bemoan the poor market. On the other hand, he too could become the victim of that dark god if he were to lose his farm or his wife or a favorite child.

If they talk about it, then they're not serious.

This is dangerous as well as false. The fact is that talking about death, "ending it all" and "not always being around" is a pretty good sign that someone is seriously considering those options. The suicidal person is ambivalent towards death, not decided upon it. They are exploring the two sides of Hamlet's question: "To be or not to be." Once they answer the question then they are either over a crisis or else set on a deadly path.

Let's suppose that their talk of suicide is not lethal. That is to say, they are really not intent on killing themselves. Such talk is pretty common. You've probably said words like that in an argument or when depressed. Should I ignore you? If you said to me: "I'd be better off dead," should I just shrug my shoulders and walk away? How would I know if you were or weren't serious? Would you say those words if you weren't angry or depressed? Aren't your feelings serious? Do you want me to take them seriously? If nothing else, people talk that way because they want to be heard.

Let's suppose that they don't intend to kill themselves but they are willing to hurt themselves to get attention. They might be willing to cut their wrists or ingest too much medicine. Isn't that serious? I once knew a man who would cut himself every year on his birthday. He was covered with big ugly scars. I met him at a mental health center after he had cut his throat with a whiskey bottle. The cut was huge and gaping but not deadly. He refused medical treatment. He didn't really want to kill himself; he wanted to punish himself. Does that mean it wasn't serious?

All talk of suicide is serious. It is the talk of someone who is hurting and in need of our help and it must always be taken seriously.

He didn't give a sign.

In virtually every suicide, the first words I've heard were, "he didn't give any sign at all that he was suicidal." The next words are usually a list of all the signs he gave. "He did say something at breakfast the other day about not being around any more." "He never really had many friends around here." "He had been a little down lately." "He was asking some really weird questions about if I thought it hurt to die."

People contemplating suicide are ambivalent. They are not totally decided to die. If they were decided then they would have already done it! They are not sure because each of us has a very strong urge to live. So even in the worst cases there are some warning signs. The problem is being aware and being there so that we can notice the signs.

"But he had cheered up in the past few days. He seemed like his old self." That too is sometimes a sign. After going through the dark trial that includes depression and withdrawal the potential suicide sometimes experiences an upswing in mood. For some it may be due to relief. They have made their decision and given in. The struggle is over. For others, perhaps it is just some sort of calm before the storm. The main signs to watch for are the changes, not necessarily the specific mood! Even professional helpers have made this error. The signs are always there. It's just that we may not be wise enough or observant enough to see them.

She just wanted attention.

This is said to minimize the seriousness of a suicide attempt. There are two things wrong with this myth. First, any suicide attempt is serious. Although mental health professionals do distinguish between an "attempt" and a "gesture," the fact is that either can result in death. In fact it seems that just crossing the barrier from thinking about suicide to acting on those thoughts is the most difficult thing for the suicidal person. Once the barrier is crossed it is much easier to try again. One of the saddest cases I witnessed was of a young woman who took about half a bottle of aspirin. In her inexperience she supposed that aspirin was not lethal! An accidental death is still a death.

The second problem with this myth is that it minimizes the need for attention. Sometimes we hear the word "manipulative" in reference to these so-called "gestures." Those who use the word "manipulative" mean to imply that there is something invalid or unreal about the cry for help. What must be realized is that all suicides are probably in some sense manipulations of other's feelings. They are cries for help. They are attempts to be noticed and included. That doesn't detract from their seriousness.

Think about it for just a moment. Someone you know slashes her wrists with razor blades. She's scarred but she lives. Or maybe he drives his car into a tree. He's hospitalized but living. That sounds serious to me. Doesn't it to you?

They can't be talked out of it.

The suicidal person is confused. Death is not the only option. He is struggling between life and death. The suicidal person is reaching out for some kind of help in that struggle. He wants direction. We might be able to offer that direction or perhaps bolster the cause of life. More importantly, we might be able to show them that someone cares.

My experience is that the person in crisis is often very open to direction and one of the best things we can do is offer that direction. I once witnessed a car wreck where a small car was overturned. The driver was still buckled in his seat. He was unconscious. His wife was hysterical. She was screaming: "You've got to help my husband." She was talking rapidly and crying. The paramedics were having a hard time because of her interference. I gently but firmly began giving her directions. "Please step over here." She came. "You want us to help your husband, don't you?" She nodded as I nodded. I began asking her questions: name, residence, husband's medical history. She answered still crying but no longer hysterical. I said: "You must be very tired." She nodded. I showed her a seat and helped her get comfortable as we reassured her about her husband. People in crisis appreciate and respond to direction.

If someone really wants to kill himself, he will.

The problem with many of these myths is that there is an element of truth in them. This myth is a corollary to the last one. It also goes hand in hand with the myth that "attention-getting" suicide attempts aren't so serious. While it may be true that a suicidal person may succeed, it is not true that a suicidal person stays suicidal all the time. They can be helped but this myth discourages us from helping. The lethal intent of a suicidal intent is all the more reason for us to help—not an excuse to do nothing.

Besides, in another sense this myth is just not true. The human body can be remarkably tough. One afternoon while working at a crisis center I took a call from a woman who said she was depressed. When I asked why, she explained that she had attempted to hang herself in her apartment but was unable to because of the structure of the rooms. She had tried to cut her wrists. She was able to cut her wrists but didn't cut deeply enough so she bled for a while but didn't die. Frustrated and depressed she went to her kitchen and tried to suffocate herself in her oven. She had just awakened before she called me. Now she was even more depressed than ever. "I can't even kill myself right." While this story may provoke a smile or even a laugh in some it should be remembered that she was in real pain.

Most cases have no room for smiles. A young man I met at a mental health center filled a plastic trash bag with gasoline, put it over his head, and lit it. He didn't die and now lives with horrible scars that cover his upper body, his face, and his hands. There are case after case of people who tried but failed and now live with scars from bullet wounds or serious internal injuries from medicines. Just because they want to kill themselves doesn't mean they'll succeed. And not succeeding doesn't mean they weren't serious.

Talking about it may plant the seed.

This may be the most insidious myth of all. Too often "suicide" is a whispered word. It is not something to be locked away in a closet. It carries no more shame than cancer or heart disease. The taboo that our culture has built around the subject has served only to increase the pain of the survivors and the guilt of those who are at risk.

There is some evidence for such things as "cluster" suicides and "copy cat" suicides. However these seem to add very little to the overall suicide rate. Clusters of suicides in a neighborhood or school sometimes occur particularly among teenagers. Factors such as survivor guilt and grief may contribute to clustering. Copy cat suicides refer to an increase in the number of suicides following the portrayal of suicide on television or in a movie. Copy-catting may be due in part to the romanticized way that suicide is often treated on film. Both contribute to the isolation and depression a potential suicide already feels but neither contributes significantly to the overall rate of suicide. Both clustering and copy-catting can be countered by some realistic caring talk.

Suicide is not contagious. Talking about it doesn't create the desire to do it. In fact just the opposite is true. By getting it out in the open we can get help to those who need it. By talking about it we can increase our ability to prevent it and to survive it. Suicide is a sinister force of darkness that does not thrive in the light.

3 The Facts About Suicide

Suicide means to kill oneself.

Now suppose that right now a terrorist drove by your house and threw a grenade into your living room. Suppose also, that I, the caring and loving mental health professional, just happen to arrive at just the right time to throw my body on the grenade and save you and all you hold dear. I'm sure that you would never forget my name but would you call me a suicide? Or would I be a hero? Somehow our definition of suicide doesn't quite fit.

In fact, it is sometimes hard to define suicide. Most would not consider the self-sacrificing hero to be a suicide. Would you want the doctors to "pull the plug" if you became brain dead with no opportunity for a continued full life? Does the decision to make out a "living will" authorizing the stop of life support make a person suicidal? Most would call that the right to die with dignity and something quite different from suicide. What about the fugitive who prefers death at his or her own hands rather than torture, abuse, or slavery? Many would consider such people to be honorable and even heroic—not at all like suicides.

So, let's look at our definition again. Suicide is the taking of one's own life because of an involuntary impulse to do so. This does not include self-sacrificing acts of heroism, the defiance of fugitives, or the desires of those who wish to die with dignity. We are also not including suicides that are prompted by hallucinations or delusions.

Risk Factors

Suicide is no respecter of persons or classes. There are, however, indicators of greater risk among some. The first big warning sign is a history of suicide attempts or gestures. It is as though that first attempt is the hardest barrier to cross. Once it is crossed, the second try becomes much easier. Most suicides have a history of two or more attempts.

Another all too obvious red light is a suicide threat. Every threat must be taken seriously. Afterall, even if it is "manipulative" as we discussed in the previous chapter, it is still a very serious cry for help.

People who are suffering from some sort of affective disorder such as clinical depression or what used to be called a manic-depressive disorder are also at greater risk. Most suicides involve symptoms of depression.

People who are undergoing serious stress are greater risks. Of course, stress is a part of our life and includes many positive things but some stresses are especially linked with higher suicide rates. People with chronic or terminal illnesses are greater risks. Those who are in bereavement, especially widows within the first year of the husband's death, have greater risk.

Of course, for most of us financial stress is one of our biggest stresses. And in fact, the suicide rate goes up during times of economic recession. Either extreme of the economic spectrum is more at risk than those in the middle. The sense of hopelessness and despair that comes with recession and a greater rate of suicides go together.

While married people as a whole have a lower suicide rate than single people, marital difficulties cause the rate to rise dramatically. One of the groups at most risk of suicide are young married couples within the first year or so of marriage. Of course, separations and divorces cause a rise in the suicide rate.

There are also other factors that can contribute to greater risk. Young people who have bad relationships or who are engaging in dangerous and illegal behaviors like alcohol and drug abuse are high risks. Young Blacks and Hispanics also have a greater than average suicide rate. So do Native Americans. Prisoners are at risk. Viet Nam veterans have a high rate of suicide. Gays and lesbians also have high rates. Middle aged men who feel that life has not been what they expected are among the greatest risks. Men generally have a higher rate of suicide than do women (nearly 4 to 1) and the rate climbs with age. Non-religious people are at greater risk than Protestants and Protestants have a greater risk than Catholics or Jews.

Even location can contribute. The suicide rate is greater in cities and lower in rural areas. At one time the highest rate in Europe was in West Berlin before the wall came down as a visual reminder of the isolation and division.

As you can see, the "at risk" groups are many and varied and the factors that can contribute to suicide cover a broad spectrum. To summarize, we can say that suicide is more likely to happen to an elderly, white, single, divorced or widowed man who isn't religious, lives in the city, and who is either very high or very low in occupational status. And it will most likely occur during a time of economic depression or recession and will take place in the early evening hours.

Causes

Many great thinkers have considered the causes of suicide. So it's not surprising that we find a number of theories about why people take their own lives. Freud theorized that there are two basic drives: a drive toward life (Eros) and a drive toward death (Thanatos). Karl Menninger proposed three motives: the wish to kill, the wish to be killed, and the wish to die. Alfred Adler said that suicide is a veiled attack on others. Jung hypothesized that suicide is a way of escape and that unconsciously the person saw death as the door to new life. Harry Stack Sullivan said that suicide is hostility toward others that is directed toward the self. Karen Horney said it was the result of personality and development. Emile Durkheim saw three types of suicide: the egoistic, the anomic, and the altruistic. The altruistic was a sacrifice for a cause. The anomic represented a failure to adjust to a great change in fortune or position. The egoistic, which he believed to be the most common, was due to alienation from others.

This is not a book of theory but it seems that at some level depression is a contributing factor to suicide. Something happens that causes depression and that in turn decreases the desire to live. Depression is associated with most cases of suicide.

On the other hand, the Thanatos of Freud and the misdirected anger of Adler and Sullivan seem to be a factor also. Suicide is a message. The primary content of the message is anger and that anger is often directed at a specific person.

A thirteen year old boy killed himself and left a note. The note said: "I am not going to kill her because I want her to see my body and realized that because she has possessed me and shut me and her in glass cases I am dead. I want her shown up for what she is—a maniac." That's anger.

The examples are many. The schoolyard killer who after shooting several children kills himself. The disgruntled federal employee who kills several others and then himself after losing his job. The twenty-three year old woman who hung herself and left this note. "I hate her and all the people who couldn't love me just for me. They would just begin to love me and then would meet her and the love for me would stop almost immediately. I am never going to let her take anyone from me again. I will stop at nothing." The man who kept his own children hostage while he spoke to his wife on the phone so she could hear the gunshots as he killed them and then himself. Anger can be a factor.

Most likely, both depression and anger are involved in every suicide. Even though it seems that there is a common thread.

The Common Thread

The factors given above cover almost everyone: young-old, black-white, rich-poor. There is, however, a common thread that runs through them all. The more isolated a person feels the more likely that person is to commit suicide. To put it another way, the more a person identifies with a group the less likely it is that that person will commit suicide. This is the factor that Emile Durkheim identified as alienation from others.

So we find the high rates among men who too often are emotionally isolated because of cultural traditions that teach them not to share their feelings and among young people who are not quite sure yet who they are and are often overly concerned with being popular. Those who have lost or have never had a significant other as a spouse are in a world alone and often lonely. Yet the greatest loneliness sometimes occurs in the young, married family where instead of oneness and love they have fear and distrust. Perhaps the large numbers of people in cities serve to emphasize a person's separateness and anonymity.

For some, their status in a group is how they define themselves. So lack or loss of economic achievement takes away people's identity especially in this society where the first question we ask people often relates to their occupational status. This may be part of the explanation for the high rates among Black and Hispanic men who also have greater than average rates of poverty and joblessness. For Native Americans, we find their identity attacked not only economically but also culturally. The rites of passage and the vision quests were ways of defining oneself within the tribe. Now for the most part these are gone and with them the sense of belonging.

This same factor seems to be why Jews and Catholics with their strong sense of ritual and cultural identity have lower suicide rates than Protestants. Most Protestant groups are much more loosely affiliated and even theologically stress the importance of the individual sometimes at a loss of a sense of community.

Isolation. Loneliness. A lack of identity with a group. This is the sad dark thread that seems to be woven into every suicide.

4 Warning Signs

Many of us watch or read a weather forecast every day. We do so because we believe that meteorologists can to some degree predict the weather. Yet few of us believe or expect the forecast to be 100 percent accurate. Even the forecaster words the predictions in terms of odds as though it were a gamble ("50 percent chance of rain"). But that doesn't mean we don't believe in weather forecasts. No indeed, we believe in them and sometimes even make plans according to them. Of course we would probably feel more confident if there were more known about the causes of weather. We'd feel better still if we knew that all those causes could be known. The more we know and the more we could find out would increase our confidence in the weather report.

That's exactly the case with suicide. No one knows all the answers. The theorists don't agree with each other. We can't know for sure what is going on in another person's head. In fact, we are not even sure what is going on inside our own heads. But we do believe that what people do can be predicted. We go on our green lights because we predict that the other guy will stop on his red light. We say words to get attention or to ask questions because we predict that others will respond. But like the weather forecasts, people predictions are not 100 percent accurate. Why? Because like the weather, we don't know enough about why things happen.

Of course, even if we knew all the causes and dynamics of why people do what they do, that doesn't mean we could predict with 100 percent accuracy. Maybe the weather in New York City tomorrow will be affected in some way because I turned my compost heap today. That might make sense according to meteorology but there's no way it could be factored into the weather report. In fact, there's no way it could even be noticed. So it is with people. We are not living in a vacuum. We are subjected to thousands of influences everyday. Then there is our personal history. And of course there are the random thoughts that come to us unexpectedly. Even if we knew everything about how people think and behave we would not be able to observe all those things.

For example, perhaps later on today or even tomorrow you will be walking across a parking lot. There you meet someone who is suicidal. How would you know? Would there be signs? Of course, just like there are fronts, barometric pressures, temperatures, and so forth, everywhere in the world for the weather forecaster. Would you notice them? Probably not, unless they were very blatant. To observe them would require you to be more familiar with that person. Then again, if you are under stress or preoccupied with some problem or task it's even less likely that you will notice what is going on with others. Does this make you a bad person? No, just a person.

In short, there are always warning signs. But even the wisest and most knowledgeable among us doesn't know enough and can't observe enough to predict everything a person will do. We cannot hold ourselves responsible for the suicide of a co-worker or family member. It is unrealistic to say to ourselves: "I should have known." We too are human with human limitations.

On the other hand, even though we can't do everything we can do something. The more we increase our understanding and awareness the more we will be able to reduce the risk of suicide. We might not be 100 percent accurate but 25 percent accuracy might be enough to save the life of someone we know and love.

Signs of Depression

As mentioned in the last chapter, depression and suicide go hand in hand. Depression is more than just being sad. It is extreme and debilitating. Following are some common symptoms of depression:

- *A change in appetite.* Most often this will be a decrease in appetite over a period of time that results in significant weight loss. It could however be the opposite—an increase with weight gain. The key word is CHANGE.

- *Physical complaints.* There may be complaints about physical symptoms, such as stomach aches, fatigue, and headaches.

- *Neglect of appearance.* The depressed person may lose interest in such things as grooming and personal hygiene.

- *Negative feelings.* There may be feelings of loneliness, worthlessness, guilt, sadness, or agitation. These may be verbally expressed or noticeable from facial expressions.
- *Lack of interest in former activities.* There may be boredom or disinterest associated with activities which the person formerly enjoyed.
- *Withdrawal or isolation.* This is a major sign for suicide as well.
- *Decreased ability to concentrate.*
- *Decreased quality of work.*
- *Moodiness.* A depressed person doesn't necessarily sit around and cry all the time. They may show abrupt anger or irritability.
- *Change in sleep patterns.* They may be unable to sleep or they may begin sleeping all the time.
- *Loss of energy.*

Situational Clues

As mentioned in the last chapter, there are factors that increase the risk of suicide. Everyone who experiences these factors doesn't become suicidal. However, even if they don't become suicidal they need our support. If we are aware and supportive, then we will more likely notice other signs if they arise. Such situational factors include economic distress, major diseases, AIDS, the death of a loved one, divorce, and other drastic difficulties.

It is in part a matter of stress. We can define stress as pressure that is put on a system. A certain amount of it is necessary. Without the stress for example, it would not be possible for an airplane to fly. By the same token, without the stress of paying bills some of us might not work at all. Without the stress of grades some students would not study. But stress is pressure and as such puts a strain on the system. If an engine is overworked, it will stop. If there is too much stress on the wing of an airplane it will crack. So it is with our systems. Too much for too long, even if we are real good at pretending that we are tough or don't care, will sooner or later cause our system to break down. This might mean physical problems (ulcers, headaches, etc.), problems at home or work, or even suicide.

We are all subject to stress. The greater the stress the greater the risk of suicide, especially if the stressors are extremely traumatic such as deaths, loss of job, and major illnesses.

Self-destructive behaviors

There are ways of killing ourselves that are not strictly suicide are dangerous and self-destructive. The suicidal person may begin to show some of these behaviors as a way of flirting with death. Just as with situational clues, these do not mean that everyone who does them is suicidal, but they are frequently signs that someone needs our support. For some they may be attempts at indirect suicide. If nothing else maybe we can find a way to share our concern without being bossy or intrusive. On the other hand, if the person is an adolescent we may need to make our values very clear.

Dangerous and self-destructive behaviors include the following:

- Alcohol abuse.
- The use of drugs (including the abuse of over-the-counter drugs).
- Eating disorders such as bulimia and anorexia.
- Promiscuous sexual activity.
- Reckless driving. There is reason to believe that a significant percentage of car accidents (especially single driver accidents) are in fact suicides.
- Illegal activities.

Major Signs

There are some signs that relate specifically to suicide. These are major indicators of the risk and the seriousness of the risk. Some of them are also included on the lists above but they seem to be especially accurate signs of suicidal risk. The more that you see, the more likely it is that not only is the person suicidal but that they have a strong lethal intent.

HISTORY OF ATTEMPTS. Most people who "succeed" at killing themselves have tried several times before. The more attempts a person has isn't a reason to discount the seriousness of their intent. It is a reason to consider them suicidal and to take seriously other signs and threats. Even if they don't intend to kill themselves they are self-destructive and could even die accidentally.

PREOCCUPATION WITH DEATH. The suicidal person will often talk, write, or draw about death. They may discuss means or ask what others think it would feel like. This preoccupation often is in the form of thoughts about suicide or a wish to be dead. There might be questions about "what you will do when I'm not here." There may be a sudden interest in a will.

LACK OF PLANNING FOR THE FUTURE. Other than preparations for death, the suicidal person has little interest in a future he or she will never see.

GIVING AWAY POSSESSIONS, especially prized possessions.

A HISTORY OF SUBSTANCE ABUSE.

A LACK OF GROUP INTEGRATION. Withdrawal from the group, lack of relationships and being the scapegoat for a group are major red flags.

AVAILABILITY OF A SUPPORT SYSTEM. The presence of a support system dramatically decreases the risk of suicide. However, this must be coupled with the person's willingness to use the support system or other resources.

PROXIMITY OF OTHERS. Being alone increases risk. Few suicides occur in public. For one thing, the people around will stop it if they can.

SLEEP PROBLEMS.

A PLAN. A clear sign of lethal suicidal intent is a definite plan. The more lethal and irreversible plan indicates greater deadly intent. The man on a ship who says he's going to kill himself by throwing himself in front of a train or by jumping off a mountain probably isn't too lethal. On the other hand, if he is purchasing guns, collecting pills or in other ways preparing to carry out his plan then we should be very concerned.

5 The Plan to W.I.N.N.

The objective of W.I.N.N. is to reduce the risk of suicide and to save lives. Because of our lack of knowledge and limitations, we will probably not be able to stop every suicide. But if you knew that your daughter or son's life was in danger what would you do to save it? If you were to see someone being murdered or raped, what would you do? What if the victim were your wife or husband? No, we may not be able to stop every suicide but what if we could stop just one?

There are suicide prevention centers and crisis lines in most major cities in the United States. These are the outgrowth of the concerns of people for people. They are often staffed by volunteers who are concerned and want to do something for others. No doubt they have been responsible for the saving of many lives through the years. The sad reality is, however, that such programs have very little effect on the suicide rate. Most of the people who call in to such lines are not suicidal. They may be depressed or worried or undergoing some crisis but most are not suicidal.

The problem with the suicide crisis line is that it is passive. Its success depends on the willingness of the suicidal person to call for help. Too often they don't call.

Perhaps they are afraid they'll be picked up by the police and locked up. Perhaps they are afraid that others will find out and they'll have to carry the stigma of being a "mental patient." Or perhaps others will consider them weak or sinful. Maybe they have lost all hope and are too far down the road to turn around.

An effective approach to combatting suicide requires a greater awareness and concern on the part of many people. It requires an attack on the roots of suicide as well as a response to the threat.

W.I.N.N. is an acronym designed to help us remember some basic ways in which we can reduce the risk of suicide among those who are closest to us. It is a practical approach that is designed to save someone's life. But it is also designed to increase our awareness of the core problem: isolation.

The plan is quite simple: Watch, Integrate/Intervene, Never, Never.

We might not be able to save everyone but we can help save someone. We might not be able to cure every problem but we might help solve one. We may not be able to rescue everyone from despair but we can include someone. That's the aim of the program that we will be discussing in the next few chapters.

6 Watch

The first step in reducing the risk of suicide is to watch. Watch what? Watch people. This is not only an important step in suicide prevention but can also be both enlightening and entertaining. Watching people is the best way to learn what people in general really do. It is also an important step in getting to know each other as individuals.

Most of what each of us does follows a pattern. That's because it's easier. We don't think before each gesture or move. Although we might think before we walk or shake hands once the decision is made the action itself is performed pretty much automatically. If we had to consciously think before each thing we did, we would find it awkward and even difficult. That's why you can psych out an opponent in baseball or golf by casually asking about their stance or their grip. The question causes them to think about something that has been automatic and unconscious. Once they think about it they mess up.

Even in other areas we are for the most part creatures of habit. We each have preferences in color, clothes, word choice and for the most part, follow our preferences.

By watching people we can pretty soon determine what their patterns are. Some smile a lot. Some frown. Some move quickly. Some slowly. Some talk more. Some talk less. These patterns of behavior are what psychologists call a "baseline." It's important to establish what a person's baseline is because otherwise we tend to judge other people's behavior by our own. If we are quiet then we might think there is something wrong with the person who talks a lot, for example. In fact, we are all different and have our own individual ways of doing and being.

Once you know what a person's baseline behavior is, then you will be able to notice when something is different. This is a major clue that something is going on inside. Remember that most of what we do is automatic. When we begin to think about it or when our emotions become so pronounced that they cause us to become self-conscious then the patterns break up. If a person who normally smiles all the time stops smiling, something must be going on. On the other hand, if a person who frowns all the time starts smiling that should cause us to wonder too. Changes in behavior are clues that a person is preoccupied with thoughts or emotions.

There are also specific signs to look for. A number of these signs were discussed in Chapter 4. They include situation clues such as recent deaths, marital difficulties, economic reversals and other major stressors. Included also are self-destructive behaviors that are not specifically suicidal: alcohol abuse, drug use, unsafe driving, illegal activities, and promiscuous sex for example.

We should particularly watch for signs of depression.

These include changes in a person's appetite and sleeping habits. A depressed person may also show a marked change in the energy level. Most will show signs of being sad or agitated. They may start neglecting things like their appearance and show less interest in their work. They may seem preoccupied. They might complain of physical complaints that relate to emotions such as headaches or stomach aches.

Specific suicidal signs to watch for include a preoccupation with death. They might draw pictures of death. They might talk or ask questions about it. They may show a sudden interest in their will. Or they might give away their most prized possessions. Almost certainly they will withdraw from others.

Remember that none of these signs alone means anything. They must all be considered together and considered in the light of how the person usually acts. It is very difficult to know what another person is thinking or feeling. Of course the more we know about them the more we can infer from their behavior, but then there are few of us that really know that much about others or even ourselves.

So what if you notice that someone seems a little withdrawn and morose. They usually smile but recently are frowning. They seem tired. You suspect that something is bothering them. You're concerned that they might be suicidal. What else can you do? The best way to find out what others are thinking is to ask them.

You can simply ask if anything is bothering them. That is a message of concern and support. You can offer them your listening ear. Each of us has times when we need another who is willing just to listen.

If you are concerned that they may be considering suicide, ask them. There's no quicker way to find out. Although many people are hesitant to bring up the subject, that's exactly what a professional does when they suspect that suicide is the issue. Asking about it does not make it more likely. In fact, asking about it makes it less likely.

The first thing that should be noted concerning talking about suicide is that virtually everyone who is depressed thinks about suicide. We don't normally admit this because of the taboos surrounding the subject. If we admit that we have thought about suicide then we are afraid that others will consider us to be "crazy." But in fact, everyone who is depressed at some time or other considers what it would be like to "end it all." That doesn't mean that we are suicidal or that we will become suicidal. It means that we are depressed and thinking depressed thoughts. For most it ends there because the life-urge is too strong.

Of course there is a right way (or at least a better way) to bring up the subject. If we say, "you're not thinking of killing yourself are you?" then we put them on the defensive. Even if they are suicidal they will be less likely to answer truthfully because we have framed our question to be negative and judgmental. It would be better to simply ask, "Have you been thinking of killing yourself?" Many of us are afraid of actually saying those words. If that is the case you might say "hurting yourself" instead of "killing yourself" and then work from there.

The very best way of asking is to point out that virtually everyone who is depressed at some time or other has thoughts of suicide. Then ask them if they have been having such thoughts. Most will sigh with relief at being able to discuss their thoughts with someone without the danger of being labeled. They probably thought they were losing their minds when in fact they were just experiencing the kind of thoughts people have when they're depressed. As they talk about it they will be able to explain their feelings and thoughts with your encouragement. Most of the time they'll say something like: "Of course I could never kill myself, I'm too much of a coward." Or, "I could never kill myself, I've got the kids." In other words, they start giving reasons for living which is exactly what we want them to do. You don't have to give them the reasons. They'll think of them themselves.

Now in the event that a person is suicidal and not merely depressed, the thoughts of suicide will be more persistent. You might want to find out more. Ask them if they have a plan. The more realistic and lethal the plan is the more at risk they are for suicide. If they plan to shoot themselves then find out if they have access to a gun. Find out how long and how often they have been thinking this way. Don't discourage them from talking by being shocked or judgmental. Just listen and encourage them to talk. The more you find out about what's going on the more you'll be able to help. In fact, the more you listen and let them talk about their feelings, the more help you are already giving.

7 Intervene and Integrate

You are aware of the people around you. You have watched and listened. You have noticed that Sally is depressed. She has lost a lot of weight because she has stopped eating. She has rings around her eyes from lack of sleep. She seems tired and withdrawn. She no longer participates in the spades game during coffee break. You overheard her talking about "getting out of this mess." In your concern you asked her if everything was alright. Her eyes watered and she said that things weren't as good as they could be. You asked if she'd like to talk; she said she would. During the course of your little talk she admitted that she had been thinking off and on of overdosing on some pills she had from an old prescription. Now what do you do?

The key is *do something*. Don't just walk away from it all and assume you have done your share by noticing something was wrong. Do what you can to save her life.

The very strongest intervention we can make is to listen and show concern. That contact with people who care is the strongest medicine we have against the loneliness and despair that goes with suicide. There is no formula to be followed for showing that we care. We each must do it in our own way with our own personalities. There are a couple of guidelines:

Don't argue with them. People are not argued out of suicide. It is not a rational decision they are making. It is an impulse—an emotional urge—over which they have little control and which they are already fighting.

Don't judge them. They already feel guilty just for having such thoughts. Preaching and moralizing will just push them away. You want to draw them closer not push them away. You want to help lift their burdens not add to them.

Don't use cliches. Cliches like "I know what you're feeling" don't make you more credible. In fact, in most cases they only serve to sever the connection.

Don't play one-up with them. They don't need to care about your tragedy and suffering. They need you to listen.

Do listen actively. To listen actively is to really try to understand what they are saying, thinking, and feeling. In most of our conversations we are more concerned with communicating *to* than *with* others. So we are often thinking of our response while they're speaking. Or we might be thinking of something totally different. To really listen takes some concentration and effort. You can improve your listening by asking clarifying questions. "Are you saying....?" They'll either correct you or agree.

They'll know you are trying to understand. Another technique is to paraphrase their words. For example:

"Everything is so hopeless."

"You are really discouraged."

"Yeah, I am."

Remember that silence is okay. Just be there. It's not so much what you say but how you say it. Just be yourself and communicate concern. Give them your full attention. Remember that you are on their side.

Deal with them not their problem. This is not the best time to give advice or to try to solve their problems. Talk about them and their feelings. Give them the support they need to find their own answers or to realize that sometimes there are no answers.

Deal with the pain. Don't try to steer the subject away from the pain. Don't let your discomfort deprive them of the opportunity to open their hearts to you.

Let them know that you don't want them to kill themselves. Don't take responsibility for them. Just let them know sincerely that you care and that you would not want them to kill themselves. If they are not seriously suicidal (they don't have a plan and they have no way to carry out a plan) then you might make them promise to call you or someone else before they do anything. The more specific you make the promise the better. If possible also have them promise to get more sleep and to get rid of anything that could be used for suicide. As strange as it sounds this is a very effective intervention.

If they have a lethal plan and are intent upon doing something, then you must do what you have to in order to save their life. This might involve calling the police and having them taken to the local crisis center.

In cases of severe depression or suicidal risk it is a good idea to seek professional help. Find a counselor that is willing to help them through this rough period.

In any case, **DO SOMETHING**. Talk, listen, refer. Show them that you care and that there is light at the end of the tunnel. Give them hope.

Integration

The single most important thing we can do to reduce the risk of suicide is to make people feel that they belong. This is because the common denominator in suicide is the feeling of isolation. When we combat that isolation, we combat suicide.

Soldiers are away from home and often in stressful and even dangerous circumstances. The majority of these soldiers are in an age group that has a relatively high rate of suicide. But despite these facts, the rate in the military is lower than the rate among their civilian counterparts. The main difference is that soldiers belong somewhere.

They have squads, platoons, and companies. Their leaders try to instill in them a sense of *esprit de corps*—a sense of pride in belonging to a group. In fact, recently the military has reported an increase in the suicide rate. This increase coincides with the forced separation from the military because of budget cuts.

Anything we can do to make someone feel a part of a group helps to decrease the risk of suicide. Love and friendship are antidotes to feelings of isolation. Families should be the first place we feel and show this kind of caring. Of course there is no reason why we cannot also show concern and love for others as well.

Another important part of integration is the forming of rules, values, and traditions. Contrary to what some misinformed people might think, rules help to make people feel as though they belong.

Parents should not hesitate to establish rules for their families. The same goes for teaching values. While it is important to teach facts and figures, knowledge seems to have little bearing on what we do. For example, teen pregnancy has continued to rise in spite of sex education and a flood of information concerning the importance of condoms and safe-sex. But the teaching of values does affect what we do. In other words, simply and directly stating that something is wrong is a more effective way of instilling a value in a child than teaching the child about the behavior. And it is certainly more important than letting the child decide "when she is old enough to decide for herself." Even more important for preventing suicide, people identify their group by a set of values.

Traditions also identify us with a group. We should take the time to celebrate our families, our community, our church, our friends, and ourselves. Birthdays, holidays, and even minor rituals like handshakes between fraternity brothers, school songs, and "inside" jokes help us feel a part of a group.

Anything you can do as a parent, a supervisor, or a friend to make someone feel that they belong will reduce the risk of suicide. Anything you can do to help a group of people feel and act like a team may help save someone's life. It can be trivial like wearing the same hats. It can be disciplinary like establishing rules. It can be as simple as "you look just like your grandpa." Or it can involve schedules, programs, and formal lessons. In any case, it should include expressions of appreciation and concern over each other's happiness and well-being.

8 Never! Never!

Although much of what I'm about to write may seem common sense to many, I have to say that these rules are more often ignored than observed. So if I seem to be condescending, please understand that I have witnessed too many tragedies to take for granted that everyone will automatically follow these rules.

Never leave them alone

If you walked into a room and found someone standing on a footstool with one end of a rope around their neck and the other end around a beam, what would you do? Would you excuse yourself because it's none of your business? ("Oh pardon me, I'll come back later.") Would you ask them to wait while you went for help? ("Stay right there. I'll be right back.") Or maybe you would explain to them that suicide was not the way and tell them that they needed to get some professional help? ("I have a number of someone you ought to talk to. You can call or go at your convenience. I'm sure it will help.") I hope you wouldn't choose any of these responses.

In one particularly sad incident, I remember a young fifteen-year-old boy who shot himself. His parents were both educated people. As such, they recognized the signs: the withdrawal, the signs of depression, the giving away of his albums, his preoccupation with death. They were sure that he was suicidal. They carefully considered what they should do. For over a week they talked to each other and considered their course of action. In fact, they were out driving around talking about what to do when their son, alone at home, shot himself.

If a person is considered to be suicidal, she or he may be taken to a hospital or mental health center. Do you know what the hospital will do? If the person is considered to be a suicide risk the hospital will assign someone to watch them. Sometimes extra help is hired to be on "suicide watch." They will go with them everywhere—the TV room, meals, even the bathroom. During the night they will probably sit in their bedroom or at least check on them every few minutes. Why do they do this? They do it because they don't want anyone to commit suicide while in their hospital. That's bad business. Oh, I'm not saying that the nurses and counselors there don't care. They do. We all do. But the fact is that in that setting they are dealing with strangers. They can't possibly care as much as you.

My point is that if it's important for a business to keep a close watch on suicide risks, then it's even more important for you. For them, it's a matter of a client or a patient. For you it's a matter of someone you know well, someone you work with, or someone you love.

Never leave someone alone who you think might be suicidal. And especially don't leave them alone with the means of doing it. Take away the pills, sharp objects, and guns. If they might jump, then don't let them near the windows or the roof. If you need help then get help.

Never ignore a threat

Every threat of suicide is serious. As we mentioned earlier, most people who commit suicide have tried two or three times before. Do you want to spent the rest of your life knowing that you could have done something but didn't because you didn't take it seriously? Are you willing to gamble with someone's life that way? But let's suppose just for the sake of argument that they aren't serious. Let's suppose that they are just saying those things to "get attention." Is there something really wrong with giving them some attention? If someone feels they must threaten suicide to get attention then the hurt must be very deep and painful. If nothing else they must be frustrated and confused. Would it hurt to give them some attention?

Never keep a deadly secret

A young man came to see me because his best friend had killed himself. As one might expect, he was sad and tearful. After a while he explained to me that it was his fault. I began to assure him that feeling guilty after the suicide of a close friend is a common feeling.

"No! You don't understand! It's my fault. He told me he was going to do it. He made me promise not to tell anyone. I could have stopped him but I didn't."

What a heavy burden to carry. The situation might arise where someone cajoles you into keeping a secret

("Promise you won't tell anyone.") and then tells you about their intent to kill themselves.

You might be afraid that if you tell you will lose that friendship. But if you don't tell, the loss could be much more painful. If you don't tell are you really their friend anyway? Does a friend willingly watch a friend die?

If the situation arises that you make such a promise, you have my permission to break it.

9 What Else Can Be Done?

By far the most important thing any of us can do to reduce the risk of suicide is to simply be aware of those around us and be available for them if they need help. We can be a little less judgmental and a little more accepting. We can be sincerely interested in other people. In other words, follow the Golden Rule and treat others the way we want to be treated.

If all of us lived lives of concern and loving service, the suicide risk might disappear. But since the world we live in is not quite so perfect those who care need to do more. And there is much more that we can do.

Virtually any worthwhile activity we can support will also reduce the risk of suicide in our community. Churches, clubs, school activities and cultural events all contribute to our well-being emotionally.

We do double service when we recruit others to become involved. Belonging is the antidote to loneliness. This gift increases ten-fold if we are involved and get others involved in helping others. Soup kitchens, tutoring, coaching, community clean-up, or any other service that takes us out of ourselves and reaches out to others does more for our self-esteem than anything else we can do.

Education

Education for suicide prevention takes two forms. The first is what we are doing here—training to increase our awareness of the problem and to develop skills for dealing with it. This sort of training is important for anyone who deals with people. In other words, it's important for all of us because we all have families, friends, co-workers, and others in our lives. It is certainly important for teachers, managers, church workers, and others who have the opportunity of working fairly close with a large number of people on a regular basis. But perhaps it's even more important for the friend or family member who is more closely acquainted and involved with certain people and for whom the tragedy would be much greater.

The other role of education in preventing suicide is the teaching of the potential suicide. This involves of course the teaching of values that we mentioned earlier. These values help to build an identity as a group. Appropriate values also build self-esteem and other emotional resources. Values should also help to prevent self-destructive behaviors.

When I was a young man, I enlisted in the United States Marine Corps. Not long after arriving at Boot Camp one of my fellow recruits attempted suicide. The next morning, the rest of us were called into the "classroom" as the little seated half-circle was called where our drill instructor gave us informal instructions. While seated on the floor, we were told that one of our fellow recruits had attempted suicide. The drill instructor sounded angry. He told us that the recruit would be coming back to the platoon and that we would treat him as one of us. "Marines don't leave their wounded behind," he said. I realize now that he was building our identity as a unit and teaching us the values of the unit. He then did something very startling. He complained about how disloyal it was to commit suicide. He warned us away from it. Then he said that if we were going to do it we should at least do it right. He actually gave us a lesson on how to cut open the veins in our arms to guarantee the maximum bleeding. He then explained the best place to put the knot if we wanted to hang ourselves.

I was shocked at the time and certainly don't recommend that kind of education to anyone. However, I can now recognize some of the method of that madness. He was teaching values and integrating us into a unit. He expressed concern but he didn't take responsibility for our individual actions. He confronted us with the brutal reality of suicide and took away any sense of romance or honor. (Of course it should also be noted that we were in a very controlled environment where it was almost impossible to be totally alone any time of the day or night.)

Education to prevent suicide should be frank and honest. It should confront the brutal finality of suicide in all its ugliness.

There is nothing wrong with actually discussing the pros and cons of suicide. In fact, it's better to openly discuss them than to let them lie unexamined and unchallenged to be fuel someday to an unholy fire. Education to prevent suicide should address at least the following points:

Suicide is not romantic. Too many people have an unreal perception of suicide that is based on novels and movies. They picture the beautiful starlet lying on the elegant postered bed with her hand decorously hanging over the side. Beneath her hand on the plush rug we see the empty vial reflecting the flames from the glowing fireplace. That's not real! De-romanticize suicide. Suicide is final. It's the end. There is no "continued next week." There is no glory to it. It has no potential. In fact, it cuts off all potential futures, careers, loves, relationships, everything.

No method is foolproof. Knives and razors leave scars which are noticeable and not easily explained away. Guns maim and cause serious damage to the brain in addition to causing scars. People can survive asphyxiation and even jumping from buildings, only to find themselves crippled for life.

Suicide leaves a mess. There is no sophisticated exit. There is blood. There are smells. There's a dead body. Often this mess must be cleaned up by someone you care about because others, even commercial cleaning companies, refuse to clean it. In fact, part of the mess of death is that the anal sphincter muscle relaxes and people literally defecate on themselves. This is not a pretty picture.

Suicide is ugly. Just telling how it is may tip the scale in favor of life for many.

The Telephone

The wonderful thing about the telephone is that it puts human contact literally within our grasp. It has two roles in suicide prevention. First, as a tool for you to use in showing concern for others. Second, as a life buoy for the suicidal.

Use the telephone. It doesn't take a lot of time or effort to make a phone call. Just a call to say hello and see how things are can work wonders. Like a smile or a hug it can be a tool of encouragement. Just that little bit of human contact might be enough to remind them that they are not alone and they do matter. The phone is a two edged sword. With one edge it allows human contact and conversation. With the other edge it allows that conversation to be safe, almost anonymous. Sometimes people can open up and let out their real feelings and thoughts on the phone when they can't in person. (Maybe you've experienced that when asking someone on a date for example.) Sometimes a phone conversation can be more intimate than in person. In any event, by placing the call you are opening that door for them.

The phone as a life buoy is the basic idea behind the suicide crisis lines that can be found in many cities. Unfortunately, these lines probably don't do that much to reduce the suicide rate because the suicidal are often hesitant to call them. Most calls on crisis lines deal with stress, relationships and non-life-threatening issues. This may be due in part to a fear of being picked up by the police or labelled crazy. This isn't to say that crisis lines don't save lives, because they do. It's just that they don't do as much as we would like to have them do. But the phone is a life buoy.

If you let people know that you care, then your phone may be the life buoy that saves a friend or loved one considering suicide. The first step is to include them and to let them know that you care and that you are available. They'll call if they need to.

If they do call, then you should use the same approach you would in person. Listen actively by asking clarifying questions and by paraphrasing. Evaluate their suicide potential and if they seem to be very lethal keep them on the phone. Hanging up and breaking contact is the same thing as leaving them alone.

If you believe them to be suicidal and they hang up, call the police. Let them know what was said and that you believe the person to be suicidal. Go over yourself if you can and it doesn't seem dangerous. (It might not be advisable to go over if they were armed and had hostages for example.)

Let them know you care. The focus, as always, is to help them find options. This might involve looking at the problem. It might involve looking at their strengths and resources. It will definitely involve listening and being there for them. Recommend a definite course of action.

Most important of all, be there for them after the phone call. Be a fair weather friend and a foul weather friend both. Follow-up and develop the relationship that grew during crisis.

10 After an Attempt

Perhaps you have seen the movie *Ordinary People*. In that movie you can see a perfect example of the difficulty people have communicating about suicide. The mother so thoroughly avoids the subject (and every other difficult emotional subject) that she forces both her husband and her son into greater isolation. She goes overboard to prove to herself and others that everything is fine when in fact it's not. That's what happens in real life.

Suicide is a difficult subject. We are afraid to ask about it. We are afraid to express our own feelings including our fears. Yet, in fact, that is exactly what we must do.

The common denominator for suicides is a feeling of isolation. Our main efforts after an attempt then must be designed to bring that person in and make them feel like part of the group. Again this can't be phoney. It has to be real. There are no formulas; we each have to do it in our own way. We might make mistakes but they'll be minor and far less hurtful than withdrawing from the person.

If you have questions, ask them. If you have feelings, express them. Be kind and courteous but don't be afraid of being frank.

Suicide is a communication. Often it is an angry communicacation aimed at one person. Look at relationships. If your relationship needs help then get help. Problems like these don't just go away. We don't outgrow them. If there is a problem with your relationship or with the relationships within the family, this is probably a good time to seek outside help.

None of us does everything for ourselves. We are dependent on others for almost everything. Few of us make our own shoes and clothes and even if we did we would depend on others for nails, leather, cloth, and thread. We depend on others for farming, medicine, mechanics, building, and so on. That's the way life is. Without that cooperation and interaction we would have to do without many things. Yet, despite our dependence and interdependence many of us feel and act as though we should never need help with our thoughts, feelings, or relationships. That's not only foolish and unrealistic, it's also arrogant. If you need help, then seek help. Don't think that you can fix a complicated system like a relationship by yourself—especially if you are part of the system.

There are a number of areas that each of us can work on to help each other following an attempt. Some of these areas might require outside help. Some of them can be worked on alone.

Self-esteem can be improved. We can help others by being accepting, positive, and loving. We can help ourselves most by helping others. If your self-esteem is low then the best thing to do is to find someone else that needs help and help them. Extending yourself is the only real way of getting away from your problems.

Use your support systems. These include social groups, friends, churches, schools, community resources. We would think a man a fool who refused to get into a life raft because someone might see him and find out he can't swim. Find out what support is there and use it.

Draw on your religious convictions. Spiritual strength and emotional strength go hand in hand. Public worship, if that is your tradition, makes us feel part of something larger than us and helps us to refocus our priorities. Meditation of the scriptures and prayer exist in every religion. They exist because they work. They comfort us and help us to center our lives on things that are most important to us. For the believer they are conduits to divine help.

Have you ever watched one of those movies about the world after an atomic holocaust or one of those disaster movies about an earthquake or a crashed plane? The world as we know it has ceased. Civilization has broken down. Only a handful of people are left. When you watch those movies who do you identify with? Do you identify with the majority that are destroyed in the beginning of the movie or even before the movie starts? No, you don't. You identify with the few that are left. You identify yourself with the survivors. You do that because we are survivors. None of us thinks of ourselves as one of the statistics. We don't expect to be the auto accident or the heart attack. We expect to live because we want to live.

We are survivors and life goes on.

One of the great things about life is that it's funny. Even in the shadow of tragedy we can get glimpses of humor. You have the ability to laugh. Be willing to use it.

11 After a Suicide

The first reaction is shock. "This couldn't have happened." This is followed by a flood of emotions. "Why? What do I do now?" Members of the family will be confused. There will be guilt, rejection, rage, hopelessness, and depression—sometimes all at once.

The pain doesn't go away quickly. It will go away but it takes time. Like a physical wound that is sharp and piercing, the pain changes with time. It may scab over and we'll pick at it until it bleeds again. Eventually the sharp pain becomes dull and someday a scar. Certain times are more painful like the throb that warns of the weather. Anniversaries are painful—especially the anniversary of the suicide.

It is important to recognize and honor grief. It is not a sign of weakness to mourn. It's a sign that we miss someone. It's not something we have to hide or fear. Accept the grief. Express it and share it with others. The only cure for grief is to grieve. And grieving must be done in your own way. Remember to watch your health. And be patient.

We need to pull together. Now is the perfect time for us to make sure that everyone knows they belong. Communicate. Share. Help each other.

Many of the same things that apply after an attempt also apply after a suicide. Work on communicating with each other. Develop self-esteem by reaching out. Develop spiritual resources by reaching up and also in. Be willing to accept help. Use your support systems and resources. Be willing to laugh.

This might also be a good time for the family (work group, class, or individual) to work on some stress management and problem solving skills. You might want to gain a little more knowledge of the grief processes. An informal group discussion or some library books might provide the information you need. Or you might want to use some community resources or a counselor.

For families, it is important to include everyone. Especially don't exclude the children. We each have our own individual way of hurting. Respect that. Share with each other. There may be times when the best gift you can give your child is your willingness to let them witness your grief. Mutual help helps both the helper and the person being helped.

This is not a good time to make decisions. Delay major decisions if at all possible. Then when decisions are made they should be made by the group not by an individual. Let every voice be heard and get a consensus. Again, remember to include the children.

Accept yourself and your weaknesses. You don't have to be strong and stoic. You don't have to know all the answers. You don't have to be able to dry every tear. It's alright for you to feel guilty or even angry. Just be honest enough to recognize what you are and give yourself the same acceptance and support that you give everyone else.

Suicide is tragic. It is an insult to life and humanity. But even from tragedy can come good things. Even this terrible tragedy need not be a total waste if just one more person can learn to reach out and make this a more loving and caring world. Perhaps, at last, that is the real way we will win against suicide.

Appendix A
Religion and Suicide

Attitudes toward suicide have differed over the ages in different cultures. In the Fiji Islands, the wives of a deceased chief would supposedly rush to kill themselves. In India, women would die on their husband's funeral pyre in the practice of suttee. Of course it should be noted that many of these widows were less than enthusiastic in their devotion to their departed husband or to the rituals of their religion.

Among some Africans, a man would avenge himself on another by killing himself. This was referred to as "killing oneself upon the head of another." Custom then required the enemy to kill himself. It is amazing the customs that we sometimes catch ourselves in.

Honor, or what some have supposed to be honor, has played a role in culturally dictated suicide among several societies. The Cheyennes allowed a man one attempt to redeem his pride after a disgrace in battle. If that attempt failed, then the only way he had to redeem himself was to kill himself. Likewise, among the Chinese, traditionally the only way for a deposed ruler or a defeated general to regain honor was to die at his own hands. And of course most people have heard of the Japanese practice of seppuku or ritual suicide following a loss of face or a broken covenant.

In the western world too, there have been those who have defended suicide as an honorable and acceptable course in some situations. But for the most part, thinkers and teachers in the western world have condemned suicide as immoral. Socrates (who was forced to drink hemlock) believed that no one had the right to take his own life until summoned by the gods. His Plato also disapproved, as did his disciple, Aristotle, who considered suicide to be cowardly and a crime against the state.

Zeno, on the other hand, believed that suicide is acceptable if it is the most reasonable course. He in fact killed himself at the age of ninety-eight. His disciple, Cleanthes, starved himself to death. The Stoics however did not teach that suicide as an impulsive act was acceptable. They believed in carefully weighing the pros and cons and then accepting the best course of action.

In general, the ancient Greeks condemned suicide. In ancient Thebes, the suicide was not given any funeral rites. In Athens, the suicide's hands were cut off and buried separately. However in some Greek cities special courts were set to hear the arguments of any who wished to commit suicide. Then, if they were granted permission, the cities would even provide hemlock for them to drink. Valid reasons were such things as physical suffering, extreme sorrow, and insanity.

The Romans considered suicide to be a crime because it hurt the government and the state. But they did respect those who chose suicide to defend their honor or a principle. Cato the Younger, for example, was acclaimed for his choosing suicide rather than life under the rule of Julius Caesar.

In more recent times, Michel de Montaigne the great essayist considered suicide to be foolish but not necessarily immoral. Kant believed suicide to be immoral because life is sacred. On the other hand, Schopenhauer taught that suicide is useless and foolish but a right. David Hume, Rousseau and Voltaire argued against the concept of suicide as a crime. And even John Donne, the English poet and clergyman, defended suicide.

But for the most part, suicide has been condemned in the west. This is true for the pagans as we have seen but even more so for the three great religions of Judaism, Christianity, and Islam.

Moslems have always condemned suicide. In addition to the reasons that are shared in common with Jews and Christians, the Moslems have a distinctive argument against suicide. Islam is submission to the will of Allah. A Moslem is someone who submits to the will of Allah. That is the core and heart of Islam. That must be understood before one can understand the teachings of the Prophet and the Koran. Suicide represents an attempt to defy destiny (kismet) or the will of God. For that reason, suicide is a sin and even in a sense a rebellion against God.

For Jews, suicide is a sin. Life is the gift of God who are we to take it away? Suicide runs counter to the sixth commandment: "Thou shalt not kill." For this reason there are those in the Judeo-Christian world who reject the idea of "Living Wills" along with mercy killing as contrary to the commandments of God. However, there is also a subtle tradition of heroic suicide. Within rabbinical lore there is a place for suicide as a way to avoid slavery, sexual abuse, or idol worship. The heroes of Masada are heroes because of their willingness to commit mass suicide rather than surrender their lives and beliefs to the Romans. At Treblinka, mass suicide was a statement of freedom, self-control, and solidarity.

Christians, like Jews, have usually condemned suicide as sin. It was condemned by St. Augustine. Suicides have been denied burial in holy ground. Their bodies have been degraded and hung on gallows to rot. Superstitions have grown up around this rejection of suicides. Some supposed that suicides became vampires. To prevent this the bodies of suicides have at times been burned at a crossroads with a stake through their hearts. This attitude became ingrained in secular laws as well as allowing for the confiscation of the property of those who committed suicide.

The Bible itself has little to say about the issue of suicide. It is mentioned without comment as something people will desire at certain times due to evil or hardships (e.g., Rev. 9:6). The devil tempts Christ to hurl himself from the top of the temple (Mt. 4:5-6; Lk 4:9-11). It recounts the suicides of a number of people, including Samson, Saul, Ahithopel, Zimri, and Judas (Jud. 16:29-30; 1 Sam. 31:4-5; 1 Chr. 10:4-5; 2 Sam. 17:23; 1 Kings 16:18; Mt. 27:5; Acts 1:18). It mentions that on occasion some people have viewed death as desirable, including Elijah, Moses,

Job, Jonah, and Paul (1 Kings 19:4; Num. 11:15; Job 3; Jonah 4:8; 2 Cor. 5:2,8)." The only Biblical prohibition of suicide that I am aware of is found in the Apocrypha in the Wisdom of Solomon 1:12-13 (New American Bible): "Court not death by your erring way of life, nor draw to yourselves destruction by the works of your hands. Because God did not make death, nor does he rejoice in the destruction of the living." Early Christians in particular, possibly because of a belief in the imminent end of the world, tended to take Paul's view that "dying is gain" (Phil. 1:20-23) due to the hardships of this world. This did not lead to wholesale suicide but it was probably part of the motivation of the martyrs who were so willing to die for their faith. It should be realized however that even the martyrs would have preferred life and many very faithful Christians escaped martyrdom by hiding. Life after all is the gift of God.

The greatest value of religion in suicide prevention is not in a theology of suicide. It is instead in the values that tend to build community and caring. The fundamental teachings of love, service, repentance, tolerance, and forgiveness are also fundamental principles for the development of healthy, balanced people. In those teachings, we find the secrets to self-esteem, healthy relationships, and overcoming guilt and pain. There is much more suicide prevention in "love your neighbor" than there is in "thou shalt not kill."

The other contribution of religion is that it creates a community of believers. The religious traditions that the faithful incorporate into their lives remind them that they belong to something greater than themselves. The eating of the seder meal for the Jew is as much a celebration of belonging and identity as it is of religion. Traditions, such as family prayers, not only increase faith but also create a sense of belonging. The same is true for all the corporate practices of religion from worship services and revivals to prayer meetings and Bible studies. The little brown church in the vale is not just a symbol of faith; it is a symbol of home.

Appendix B
Assessing Risk

THE MORE QUESTIONS THAT CAN BE ANSWERED
"YES," THE GREATER THE RISK OF SUICIDE.
ESPECIALLY TAKE NOTE OF ITEMS
MARKED WITH AN ASTERISK.

*1. Is there a history of previous attempts?

2. Are they having problems sleeping or have they been sleeping more than usual?

*3. Do they have a plan?

*4. Is the plan deadly and workable?

*5. Do they have a lot of time alone?

*6. Have they been giving their prized possessions away?

7. Do they have a history of substance abuse?

8. Do they have a history of treatment for mental or emotional problems?

*9. Are they isolated from support systems?

10. Do they have limited resources?

11. Has there been a dramatic shift in the quality of their work at school or on the job?

12. Has there been a marked change in their social behavior?

13. Has their daily behavior changed (this could include things like extreme fatigue, boredom, decreased appetite, preoccupation or the inability to concentrate)?

*14. Are they preoccupied with thoughts of death?

*15. Have they recently suffered unusual stress (e.g., death of loved one, financial reversal, loss of job, etc.)?

ANY YES ANSWER MEANS THAT THEY NEED YOUR SUPPORT AND HELP. ANY YES ANSWER TO AN ASTERISKED QUESTION IS VERY SERIOUS.

OTHER FINE BOOKS FROM R&E ! ! !

W.I.N.N. AGAINST SUICIDE by Robert E. Nelson Jr. Every family in this country will be touched by suicide or the threat of suicide at one time or another. In most cases, this tragedy can be prevented, if you know the warning signs. This guide may help save someone you love. Included is information on why suicide is so common, the warning signs of potential suicide, the causes of suicide and how to reduce the risk of suicide.

$6.95   ISBN 1-56875-049-8   Order #049-8

BECOMING THE ME I WANT TO BE: A Self-Help Guide to Building Self-Esteem by Don G. Simmermacher. Everything that you do in life, from the amount of money you make to the person you marry, is determined by your self-esteem and self-image. It is believed that most of us use less than 10% of our true potential, and that if we learned how to tap into it we could transform our lives. This book will help you discover and develop a more powerful sense of self to help change your life dramatically.

$9.95   ISBN 1-56875-055-2   Order #055-2

THE POWER OF POSITIVE EDUCATION by Will Clark. Our education system is failing our children. It is not preparing them to succeed in a world which is growing increasingly more complex and demanding. Instead of helping children to become motivated learners, we are teaching them to be irresponsible and destructive. This book offers a new model and a new hope. It teaches parents, educators, political and business leaders how to work together to provide our children with the education they need and deserve.

$9.95   ISBN 1-56875-057-9   Order #057-9

THE WINNING FEELING by John R. Kearns & Garry Shulman. Most children idolize athletes. Now, there is a book that teaches how to apply the success for techniques of world class athletes toward academics. After spending years coaching some of the world's greatest athletes, and coaching their coaches, the authors have created a program that teaches students of all ages to become winners in the classroom. The authors have conducted over 300 workshops on enhancing self-esteem, the essential element in all success. Their "Winning Feeling" program has been successfully implemented in Canadian classrooms for four years.

$9.95   ISBN 1-56875-057-9   Order #057-9

TALKING JUSTICE: 602 Ways to Build & Promote Racial Harmony by Tamera Trotter & Jocelyn Allen. It is said that a journey of a thousand miles begins with a single step. This important new book is a map to the small steps that each of us can take on the path to ending prejudice and hatred. We can use these methods to bridge the gap that exists between us and members of other races. With each small, tenuous action we take, we are that much closer to understanding each other. This simple yet profound guide is ideal for teachers, clergy and individuals who want to end the hatred and venture into a strange, but beautiful new land of harmony and cooperation.

$6.95   ISBN 0-88247-982-2   Order #982-2

OTHER FINE BOOKS FROM R&E ! ! !

W.I.N.N. AGAINST SUICIDE by Robert E. Nelson Jr. Every family in this country will be touched by suicide or the threat of suicide at one time or another. In most cases, this tragedy can be prevented, if you know the warning signs. This guide may help save someone you love. Included is information on why suicide is so common, the warning signs of potential suicide, the causes of suicide and how to reduce the risk of suicide.

$6.95   ISBN 1-56875-049-8   Order #049-8

BECOMING THE ME I WANT TO BE: A Self-Help Guide to Building Self-Esteem by Don G. Simmermacher. Everything that you do in life, from the amount of money you make to the person you marry, is determined by your self-esteem and self-image. It is believed that most of us use less than 10% of our true potential, and that if we learned how to tap into it we could transform our lives. This book will help you discover and develop a more powerful sense of self to help change your life dramatically.

$9.95   ISBN 1-56875-055-2   Order #055-2

THE POWER OF POSITIVE EDUCATION by Will Clark. Our education system is failing our children. It is not preparing them to succeed in a world which is growing increasingly more complex and demanding. Instead of helping children to become motivated learners, we are teaching them to be irresponsible and destructive. This book offers a new model and a new hope. It teaches parents, educators, political and business leaders how to work together to provide our children with the education they need and deserve.

$9.95   ISBN 1-56875-057-9   Order #057-9

THE WINNING FEELING by John R. Kearns & Garry Shulman. Most children idolize athletes. Now, there is a book that teaches how to apply the success for techniques of world class athletes toward academics. After spending years coaching some of the world's greatest athletes, and coaching their coaches, the authors have created a program that teaches students of all ages to become winners in the classroom. The authors have conducted over 300 workshops on enhancing self-esteem, the essential element in all success. Their "Winning Feeling" program has been successfully implemented in Canadian classrooms for four years.

$9.95   ISBN 1-56875-057-9   Order #057-9

WALKING JUSTICE: 602 Ways to Build & Promote Racial Harmony by Tamera Trotter & Jocelyn Allen. It is said that a journey of a thousand miles begins with a single step. This important new book is a map to the small steps that each of us can take on the path to ending prejudice and hatred. We can use these methods to bridge the gap that exists between us and members of other races. With each small, tenuous action we take, we are that much closer to understanding each other. This simple yet profound guide is ideal for teachers, clergy and individuals who want to end the hatred and venture into a strange, but beautiful new land of harmony and cooperation.

$6.95   ISBN 0-88247-982-2   Order #982-2

THE ABC'S OF PARENTING: Keep Your Kids in Touch and Out of Trouble by Joan Barbuto. Raising children in our society is more difficult than ever before. This book gives parents the practical tools they need to raise responsible, capable and well-adjusted children. It teaches parents the 20 rules of discipline they must know and apply and how to avoid the types of discipline that are ineffective and psychologically damaging.

$14.95
Soft Cover

ISBN 1-56875-062-5
Order #062-5

TAKING CHARGE: A Parent and Teacher Guide to Loving Discipline by Jo Anne Nordling. At last, here is a book that shows both parents and teachers everything they need to know to discipline children effectively and fairly.

This easy-to-understand action guide will show you how to handle the most critical disciplinary issues in teaching and raising children.

$11.95
Trade Paper

ISBN 0-88247-906-7
Order #9906-7

IMAGINATIVE HEALING: Using Imagery for Growth and Change by Norman G. Middleton. Medical researchers and doctors are continually verifying the power of the mind to heal the body. This book provides specific techniques for utilizing the power of visualizaiton to create mental and physical well-being, and for encouraging spiritual growth.

$11.95   ISBN 1-56875-043-9   Order #043-9

YOUR ORDER

ORDER #	QTY	UNIT PRICE	TOTAL PRICE

Please rush me the following books. I want to save by ordering three books and receive FREE shipping charges. Orders under 3 books please include $2.50 shipping. CA residents add 8.25% tax.

SHIP TO:

(Please Print) Name: _____

Organization: _____

Address: _____

City/State/Zip: _____

PAYMENT METHOD

☐   Enclosed check or money order

☐   MasterCard   Card Expires _____   Signature _____

☐   Visa

Bob Reed • R & E Publishers • P.O. Box 2008 • Saratoga, CA 95070 • (408) 866-6303

DATE DUE			
DEC	FEB 27 2007		
NOV 11 '95	AUG 22 2008		
JUL 20 '96	DEC 10 2008		
MAY 26 '97	MAY 7 2010		
DEC 15 '97			
JUN 11 '00			
MAY 18 '00			
DEC 21 2001			
DEC 19 2003			